These questions are answered by:

____

____

____

All your answers are not wrong
All your answers are not always right
All come from your bright or dark thoughts
All come truly, deeply from your heart and soul
And all come to define who you are at this very moment

DAY 1

How would you change your approach to life?

DAY 2

What do you hate most about your work?

DAY 3

What's the worst thing you've heard in your life?

DAY 4

What helps you survive during these challenging times?

DAY 5

What is the one thing all children do perfectly?

DAY 6

If you could teach someone how to speak, would you and why?

DAY 7

How would you describe the feeling of being fulfilled, comforted, refreshed?

DAY 8

Tell me about one of the kindest things you have ever done.

DAY 9

What do you feel when you read?

DAY 10

Pretend that you're a part of a band. What do you want to call your first album?

DAY 11

Do you always wish it was any other way? Why?

DAY 12

List of things that you found objectionable

DAY 13

Has life been challenging for you at all? Why?

DAY 14

How do you deal with people who want to hurt you?

DAY 15

What do you think the future of fiction will be?

DAY 16

Will this time be different? Why?

DAY 17

Do you prefer to dance or to walk around? Why?

DAY 18

Have you made any changes in your life? What were the changes?

DAY 19

What's your favorite genre of music? (pop, rock, country)

DAY 20

List of things that don't make any sense

DAY 21

What do you find as your biggest shortcoming?

DAY 22

Why do you want to change?

DAY 23

What causes you to get excited about your work?

DAY 24

If you could be the one person to tell the story of how you started on the right path in life, what would that be?

DAY 25

What is the most significant thing you have learned today?

DAY 26

Did you do it both ways?

DAY 27

Say something about how you have your best day at work

DAY 28

How do you deal with the fact that people don't get what you're doing?

DAY 29

List of things that should not be charged

DAY 30

Tell about the strangest food you have ever eaten.

DAY 31

What do you consider beautiful? Write about it.

DAY 32

What would you do if you found yourself trapped in an elevator with seven dwarves?

DAY 33

If you could have an unlimited number of clothes, what would each make you feel more comfortable?

DAY 34

How do you respond if he/she says no?

____

____

____

____

____

____

DAY 35

Are you willing to lose a lot of sleep? Why? Why not?

____

DAY 36

Why would you rather be wrong than right?

DAY 37

What do you intend to do now?

DAY 38

What food are you most afraid of eating?

DAY 39

How would you define "success" for yourself?

DAY 40

Is there anything in your experience that doesn't make sense to you?

DAY 41

Did you figure out what's really happening? How?

DAY 42

Who do you think has the potential to do what you've been doing for decades?

DAY 43

Tell me about what can make you retreat from pursuing your goals and dreams?

DAY 44

List of things that you want to know without telling your partner

DAY 45

What would you like to see become?

DAY 46

What's your guilty pleasure?

DAY 47

Say something about what's going on here.

DAY 48

What would you do if a friend didn't tell you a secret that you wish to hear?

DAY 49

What was the first book that you remember reading?

DAY 50

What is the worst thing that you can think of?

DAY 51

How would you go about getting your cake?

DAY 52

Would you enjoy having it right in front of you?

DAY 53

What does your daughter look for in a friend?

DAY 54

What did you teach your children about compassion?

DAY 55

Do you feel good when you're feeling stressed? Why?

DAY 56

*How do you deal with the constant pressure of being on top of
the world?*

DAY 57

What is something that everyone looks stupid doing?

DAY 58

What is the one thing that you regret most about life today?

DAY 59

List of things that didn't happen

DAY 60

How do you like your coffee?

DAY 61

How can the kids learn about the world in school?

DAY 62

How would you describe the feeling of being tossed around?

DAY 63

Do you ever feel sad that you don't do more? Why?

DAY 64

Talk about your last kiss

DAY 65

What's one thing you do in the city that no one knows about?

DAY 66

Are you not afraid to take risks? Why?

DAY 67

How do you deal with what are you calling an alien?

DAY 68

What is the one thing you always wish you had more freedom to do?

DAY 69

Do you get to choose which projects you take on? Why?

DAY 70

If you had to choose one thing you could never lose, what would it be?

DAY 71

Would you rather be poor and attractive or rich and ugly? Why?

DAY 72

Is it always wrong to lie? When (if ever) is it okay?

DAY 73

What is the meaning of your name? Are you happy with it? Why?

DAY 74

What causes you to fall asleep?

DAY 75

What is the most important thing you can give your future self?

DAY 76

What would you want to be free of?

DAY 77

Tell me about the next big step you are going to take towards your dreams.

DAY 78

What do you think about yourself?

What do you dislike about your favorite TV show/book/movie/ etc?

Would you rather have your money and freedom and not be asked to make a decision for yourself?

What was the biggest victory you've won?

DAY 82

What's your online search history look like now?

DAY 83

How do you make moves?

DAY 84

Who was the person who broke your heart the most?

DAY 85

If TV didn't exist, what would you do with your time?

DAY 86

What do you think about the amount of violence on movies?

DAY 87

If you had to choose a superpower to apply to your life, what would you choose?

DAY 88

What is your greatest fear? What's your plan to overcome it?

DAY 89

What is one thing you would like to see the world change about you?

DAY 90

How do you deal when people make fun of you?

DAY 91

List of things that can leak

DAY 92

What is the one thing you wish people would understand about you?

DAY 93

What is one thing you have in common with your spouse/ partner/friend?

DAY 94

What is the one thing that looks good in front of the car?

DAY 95

What are your five favorite television programs?

DAY 96

If you had to choose one thing from your life right now that you would change for the better, what would it be and why?

DAY 97

How would you describe the feeling of being knocked out by your own excitement?

DAY 98

List of things that piss me off

DAY 99

What's your favorite stereotype?

DAY 100

Can you buy happiness? How?

DAY 101

What was the last thing you drank?

DAY 102

Where do you want to be? What do you want to do with your life?

DAY 103

When was the last time you cried?

DAY 104

If you had to choose one thing to improve the most, what would you choose?

DAY 105

Would you be able to tell if time had been altered in some way? How?

DAY 106

What is one thing you hope to achieve with your life?

DAY 107

How do you deal with people who just hate?

DAY 108

Describe a time when your quick thinking saved the day.

DAY 109

How can you stop fighting and start loving?

DAY 110

If you could, would you go back in time and do something differently from what you were doing?

DAY 111

What's the thing you wish you could make yourself laugh most?

DAY 112

Will you have anything similar in mind?

DAY 113

How would you describe the feeling of being in the presence of the gods?'

DAY 114

If you could be in a movie, what would it be?

DAY 115

If you could have any animal in the world as a pet, where would you get it and what would it be?

DAY 116

What is the one thing that's going to make you feel truly comfortable and at ease when you are wearing a suit/dress?

DAY 117

What if a cat appears in your doorstep? What would you do?

DAY 118

Would you rather never play or always lose? Why?

DAY 119

What is the most surprising thing you have learned?

DAY 120

If your friend told you of a secret plan to run away from home, what would you do and why?

DAY 121

Would you rather hear about her or him?

DAY 122

What did you do before that made you angry, sad and scared at the same time?

DAY 123

What is the most significant thing you have learned in your professional life?

Explain how different modern life would be without computers.

If you could take out all the things you can't manage, everything you hate about yourself, every thought that makes you uncomfortable, what's it going to be like to go back and live with the past?

Do you have good manners? Why?

DAY 127

What effects does cigarette and alcohol advertising have on young people?

DAY 128

What do you do when they ask you for a favor but you don't want to do it because you already know what will be result?

DAY 129

How many times did you do less?

DAY 130

List of things that you will be taking a long time to hunt down

DAY 131

Which body type do you find most appealing?

DAY 132

What is one thing you have in common with the people whom you will try the hardest to please?

DAY 133

What is the one thing that will give up your love?

DAY 134

What's the worst thing in life?

DAY 135

What is your perfect book title to describe your life so far?

DAY 136

What are you willing to accept you will never change?

DAY 137

If you were to die tomorrow, what would you want your legacy to be?

DAY 138

How do you keep your emotions in check?

DAY 139

If you had to choose one thing you would want to do if you were forced to choose from all the options presented by life, what would it be?

DAY 140

Where would you rather be from?

DAY 141

Would you rather not think about it?

DAY 142

How would you describe the feeling of the last two years?

DAY 143

List of things that can kill you

DAY 144

What do you dream about at night?

DAY 145

What kind of trophy would you like to win?

DAY 146

What would be your ideal scenario in your life?

DAY 147

What can you do to help a project?

DAY 148

Do you feel like you are good at everything you do? Why?

DAY 149

What is the one thing that you regret most about your time?

DAY 150

How do you deal with feedback?

DAY 151

What would you learn from what you do now to improve your performance?

DAY 152

What are you afraid of? Why?

DAY 153

Where are your family members from?

DAY 154

Tell about a time when you were grounded.

DAY 155

What is one thing you can change if you could choose to do one thing over?

DAY 156

What is most important to you to whom do you offer the greatest amount of attention, care, concern, and compassion?

DAY 157

What would you do if you were in the middle of the lake and your boat began to leak?

DAY 158

List of things that can make you ill

DAY 159

Would you rather have good ideas come out of nowhere? Why?

DAY 160

What is the nicest thing someone could say about you?

DAY 161

Which quality do you dislike most about yourself—laziness, selfishness or childishness and why?

DAY 162

What did you learn from your mother?

DAY 163

How do you help your daughter/son feel comfortable around others?

DAY 164

What did you learn this year?

DAY 165

Do you have to think about it?

DAY 166

How would you describe the feeling of being a part of the team?

DAY 167

What's the worst thing you've ever done in your life?

DAY 168

If you could pick one piece of clothing, what would it be and why?

DAY 169

Talk about something black that you like.

DAY 170

Write about a time in your life when the content of your character was tested.

DAY 171

Tell me 5 good things about yesterday.

DAY 172

When was the last time you were able to feel the thrill of the hunt?

DAY 173

If you could know the absolute and total truth to one question, what question would you ask?

DAY 174

What were the most interesting things about your own development?

DAY 175

What would you say if I told you that you could have something much bigger and better than you have now?

DAY 176

How would you describe the feeling of being increasingly lost in your thoughts?

DAY 177

If you could give an amazing speech to the government, what would be the topic?

DAY 178

How do you deal with people who can't understand how bad it's going to get?

DAY 179

How would you describe the feeling of being a part of something huge?

DAY 180

Who is the best live act you've seen in person and why?

DAY 181

Where do I start?

DAY 182

What is the one thing that makes everyone else a little bit crazy?

DAY 183

Who are the people in your life to whom you have to be most honest?

DAY 184

*Do your family members worry about you spending more time
on your project? Why?*

DAY 185

What would you trade for your hands?

DAY 186

Who do you think knows you best?

DAY 187

How do you deal with a situation where there are hundreds of people doing some crazy stuff that's causing problems?

DAY 188

How did you make up your mind to change when no one was listening?

DAY 189

Which language do you speak best? Why?

DAY 190

List of things that interfere with you

DAY 191

Why do you think that?

DAY 192

What's your favorite takeaway?

DAY 193

What is the worst thing you ever did?

DAY 194

What is one thing that makes you want to change something about yourself?

DAY 195

If you were going to have a nickname, what would it be?

DAY 196

What's your first reaction when you start to use your new powers?

DAY 197

What's the best way you would get the word out of the public?

DAY 198

If you had to choose one thing to do today, what would it be?

DAY 199

Many people believe that hatred is our most destructive emotion. Describe your experience that proves this statement to be true.

DAY 200

Can you describe what you experienced? Why or why not?

DAY 201

How are your mother and grandmother alike?

DAY 202

What did you say at the beginning of your conversation?

DAY 203

How could you keep your emotions under wraps?

DAY 204

Where's your favorite place to hang out?

DAY 205

What's your biggest challenge to success?

DAY 206

Will you be able to keep up with this game? How?

DAY 207

Why do you feel like a stranger?

DAY 208

How do you keep your mind healthy?

DAY 209

What are the three things you use a lot of?

DAY 210

Are you satisfied with what you're doing? Why?

DAY 211

What do you enjoy doing the most?

DAY 212

What would you miss the most if you couldn't travel?

DAY 213

What is the one thing you take away from this book that you can use to make better decisions?

DAY 214

List of things that make you loose control

DAY 215

What could you bring to the world that would make it better for those who come into contact with you?

DAY 216

What does the color Periwinkle remind you of?

DAY 217

What is the craziest thing someone told you that you now wish you had not remembered?

DAY 218

What's your favorite joke?

DAY 219

What's the worst thing you saw in the last four years?

DAY 220

What would you prefer to be called?

DAY 221

Would you rather get to the root of the issue than to take the easy way out and say "No"?

DAY 222

What do you most treasure?

DAY 223

*It is often said that animals are humans' best friends.
Describe a time in your life when this saying proved to be true.*

DAY 224

Could you save it for a rainy day? Why?

DAY 225

What do you think is your sexiest feature?

DAY 226

How can you know if you're doing this right?

DAY 227

Have you been overwhelmed lately with projects?

DAY 228

When was the last time you saw your own shadow in the mirror?

DAY 229

What are you proud of most?

DAY 230

If you could have one change to your body to change how you're seen, what would it be?

DAY 231

Throughout our lives we may be asked to do things we do not want to do. Tell about a time when this happened to you.

DAY 232

How do you think your life has been going this year?

DAY 233

What do you see as the biggest challenge going forward?

DAY 234

What are the things that you dislike the most about yourself?

DAY 235

Are your children being taught to be good listeners? How?

DAY 236

Do you prefer to be in the world before you or do you want to be in the world after you?

DAY 237

What is the one thing you can't change about your physicality?

DAY 238

Do you like getting dressed? Why?

DAY 239

Do you usually follow your heart or your head? Why?

DAY 240

Explain the meaning of diversity.

DAY 241

Would you rather be here today (where you are right now) or would you rather be here 20 years from now?

DAY 242

What has been your greatest experience?

DAY 243

How do you handle frustration?

DAY 244

Create your alter ego. What would your name be?

DAY 245

If you had to choose a weapon for a fantasy fight, which one would it be?

DAY 246

How would you describe the feeling of being drunk?

DAY 247

If you had to choose one characteristic that best represents your younger self, what would it be?

DAY 248

What's the first thing you'd like to do when you grow up?

DAY 249

If money were no object, what would you do with your life?

DAY 250

What's the most important fact in your life right now?

DAY 251

What is the one thing you're grateful for each day?

DAY 252

Where is your favorite place to live?

How would you describe the feeling of being completely in tune with your emotions?

What would you prefer to see on your resume?

How would you describe the feeling of momentum?

DAY 256

What is bad timing for you?

DAY 257

When was the first time you said you really loved someone?

DAY 258

Why do you feel so confident in your story?

DAY 259

When was the last time the two of you were on the same island?

DAY 260

What was your earliest dream job?

DAY 261

What are your hopes for a successful weekend?

DAY 262

What advice would you give to others looking to improve their lives?

DAY 263

How would you describe the feeling of pure conquest?

DAY 264

Why is it important to be honest?

DAY 265

What were the most important factors that influenced your decision?

DAY 266

Why do you think you have to want to forget your past?

DAY 267

Do you get any pleasure from reading or doing other things? Why or why not?

DAY 268

What is one thing you did this year that really made an impact?

DAY 269

What's a good thing you should be good at?

DAY 270

How do you deal with these unexpected challenges?

DAY 271

If you could use one word to describe yourself, what would it be?

DAY 272

Are you able to understand the bond between two people and their connection to each other? Why?

DAY 273

List of things that I want to do to make money

DAY 274

What are you so afraid of?

DAY 275

Who is your favorite animated character?

DAY 276

If you had to write your life story, what would the title be? Why?

DAY 277

Do you still have goals and ambitions that you want to accomplish now that you're the age that you are? What are those?

DAY 278

What has been the best and worst day so far?

DAY 279

How can you teach your children to respect themselves?

DAY 280

What gives you the most drive to get your job done?

DAY 281

How would you describe the feeling of being degraded?

DAY 282

Why do you always have to explain what's wrong?

DAY 283

List of things that I want to work on in the near future

DAY 284

What is the one thing you think everyone else doesn't get?

DAY 285

If you had to choose one thing that most bothered you, what would it be?

DAY 286

*Have you ever swallowed something and never felt the need to
go to the toilet?*

DAY 287

Who is the best laundry folder in the family?

DAY 288

What's the worst part about it?

DAY 289

Would you rather fight a dragon or a giant? Why?

DAY 290

How do you know what is real and what isn't?

DAY 291

*If you had to choose one thing to focus on to achieve your
goals, what would it be and why?*

DAY 292

What is the one thing the media cannot get away with?

DAY 293

What is your favorite second chance movie?

DAY 294

What causes you to feel this way?

DAY 295

Who do you think you are?

____

____

____

____

____

DAY 296

How would you describe the feeling of being forced to feel something you didn't want to feel?

____

____

____

____

____

DAY 297

What is one thing that was on your list of things to change?

____

____

____

____

DAY 298

When was the last time you broke someone's heart?

DAY 299

Why would you rather be angry with your parents for just allowing you to be you and proud of who you are than to have to put on a show every time you want to deal with your interdependence issues?

DAY 300

How many hours of practice a day do you have?

DAY 301

What do you think about when you get tired?

DAY 302

What is your favorite kind of lunch?

DAY 303

What is the one thing you can depend on in life?

DAY 304

What are our "fantasy solutions"?

DAY 305

What are you prepared to give?

DAY 306

How do you love to read books?

DAY 307

Why don't you share the things you've done with your friends?

DAY 308

Say something that happened that is still happening in the present.

DAY 309

What's priceless in your life?

DAY 310

Would you rather have them do it or have one do it for you?

DAY 311

What is the one thing that you plan to do now that makes you feel more confident about the future?

DAY 312

List of things that make you exceptional

DAY 313

If you could do it in the future, would you do it differently?

DAY 314

What was your worst accomplishment?

DAY 315

Who do you think was the biggest influence on you personally?

DAY 316

Tell about a time when you also chose the less-traveled path.

DAY 317

*Tell about a time when you broke the rules and what happened
as a result.*

DAY 318

*If you could pick anyone to be your life partner and they could
make your marriage better, who would it be?*

DAY 319

List of things that could cause an error either trivial or serious

DAY 320

If you had to choose one thing that is a common theme for any of your favorite books that you've read, which one would you pick?

DAY 321

Is there anything else you'd like to say? What is it?

DAY 322

If you had to choose one thing that makes your life better today, what would it be?

DAY 323

What do you want to improve upon?

DAY 324

What would your perfect room look like?

DAY 325

What is one thing that most people hate about you?

DAY 326

What are your happy days like?

DAY 327

How do you feel about the fact that the world will always be connected?

DAY 328

Say something about the game you enjoy?

DAY 329

What is the one thing you hate about your job?

DAY 330

What is the one thing that is NOT discussed here?

Are you politically inclined? Why?

If you could do one thing to improve the world, what would it be?

What color makes you think of happiness?

DAY 334

Do you have any goals? What are those?

DAY 335

If you were to change one thing about you, what would it be?

DAY 336

What is the one thing you've never been able to have in your life?

DAY 337

Would you rather have him/her or not

DAY 338

What do you want your list of achievements to have been?

DAY 339

How do you deal with people not getting it?

DAY 340

When was the last time you saw a movie that really changed your view on life? What movie was that?

DAY 341

List of things that could be different

DAY 342

Talk about someone you liked and never thought you would like.

DAY 343

Do you have a fear of doing the wrong thing? Why?

DAY 344

List of things that seem to be influenced by you

DAY 345

Which artist or writer inspires you?

DAY 346

List of things that can be seen in the room

DAY 347

Would you rather be the one doing the thinking or the one doing the doing?

DAY 348

Would you break the law to save someone you love? Why?

DAY 349

What can you do to make your work stand out, despite its limitations?

DAY 350

Have you started dating now/again?

DAY 351

If you could only have one thing on Earth, what would it be and why?

DAY 352

Should you go down a road you haven't tried before? Why or why not?

DAY 353

How would you describe the feeling of being creeped out because you're in danger?

DAY 354

If you could stop having one impulse for a while, what would it be?

DAY 355

Are you on time for this? How early? How late?

DAY 356

If you had to choose one thing in your life to live for, what would it be?

DAY 357

When was the last time you felt loved?

DAY 358

How would you describe the feeling of being discovered?

DAY 359

If you could pick just one person to be your coach, who would it be and why?

DAY 360

Would you rather eat ice cream or jelly?

DAY 361

What makes you stand out?

DAY 362

There seems to be this energetic war between your inner and outer self. Which is stronger? Why?

DAY 363

What have you done that was out of character?

DAY 364

What can you do to protect yourself?

DAY 365

What is the most significant change in your opinion?

DAY 366

If you had to choose one thing you wanted to be when you grew up, what would it be and why?